I KNOW WHAT TO DO! SOCIAL SKILLS

HOW TO SPEAK UP

CAITIE MCANENEY

PowerKiDS press.

Published in 2025 by The Rosen Publishing Group, Inc.
2544 Clinton Street, Buffalo, NY 14224

First Edition

Editor: Caitie McAneney
Book Design: Rachel Rising

Photo Credits: Cover, p. 1 areetham/Shutterstock.com; pp. 4, 6, 8, 10, 12, 14, 16, 18, 20, 21 Cute art/Shutterstock.com; p. 5 Parinussa Revy/Shutterstock.com; p. 7 Larysa Dubinska/Shutterstock.com; p. 9 DimaBerlin/Shutterstock.com; p. 11 TinnaPong/Shutterstock.com; p. 13 PeopleImages.com - Yuri A/Shutterstock.com; p. 15 AnnaStills/Shutterstock.com; p. 17 Lysenko Andrii/Shutterstock.com; p. 19 Gro[illegible]d Picture/Shutterstock.com; p. 21 wavebreakmedia/Shutterstock.com.

Some of the images in this book illustrate individuals who are models. The depictions do not imply actu[illegible] situations or events.

Library of Congress Cataloging-in-Publication Data
Names: McAneney, Caitie, author. Title: How to speak up / Caitie McAneney. Description: Buffalo, N[illegible] : PowerKids Press, 2025. | Series: I know what to do! social skills | Includes index. Identifiers: LCCN 2024033150 (print) | LCCN 2024033151 (ebook) | ISBN 9781499450606 (library binding) | ISBN 9781499450590 (paperback) | ISBN 9781499450613 (ebook) Subjects: LCSH: Assertivene[illegible] (Psychology)–Juvenile literature. | Social skills–Juvenile literature.; Classification: LCC BF575.A85 M35 [illegible]025 (print) | LCC BF575.A85 (ebook) | DDC 158.2–dc23/eng/20240725 LC record available at https[illegible]/lccn.loc.gov/2024033150 LC ebook record available at https://lccn.loc.gov/2024033151

Manufactured in the United States of America

CPSIA Compliance Information: Batch #CWPK25. For Further Information contact Rosen Publishing at 1-800-237-[illegible]932.

CONTENTS

You Have a Voice

It can be hard to speak up. You might have a lot on your mind. But you don't know how to tell someone. You might think no one cares what you say. You have a voice. You can use it to help yourself and others!

What Do You Think?

Your thoughts are important. They give you an idea of what you like and don't like. For example, you might play soccer. Maybe you don't like it anymore. You can tell your parents. Be honest. They can help you figure out what to do.

Standing Up

You can stand up for yourself. Someone might be mean to you. You can tell that person you don't like how they're treating you. You can tell a parent or teacher. You may see someone **bully** a friend. You can stand up for them too.

What You Believe

Your values are what you believe in. You may believe that people should be kind to one another. You may believe in **protecting** plants and animals. Stand up for what you believe. You can also listen to others. Your values may change over time.

What You Need

It can be hard to ask for what you need. Maybe you're scared someone will say no. However, it's important to speak up. Tell people what you need. Tell your teacher if you need more time on a test. Tell your parents if you need help.

Feelings

What you feel is important. You might feel sad. You might feel mad. These big feelings might be hard to **express**. You can speak up. You can say what makes you happy, sad, or mad. For example, "When you call me that name, it makes me sad."

Talking It Out

You can talk about your thoughts and feelings. You can tell a friend. You can tell a parent. You can tell a teacher or coach. Some people go to a **therapist** to talk. A trusted adult can help with most problems. A friend can make you feel less alone.

Speaking with Confidence

How can you express yourself? You can say, write, or draw what you think or feel. Speak with **confidence**. You can raise your hand or say "excuse me" to get someone's attention. Make **eye contact**. Raise your voice enough so people can hear it. Tell the truth.

You Can Speak Up!

If you believe in something, you can stand up for it. If something doesn't feel right to you, you can speak up about it. You can use your words to give **consent** or say no. Your thoughts and feelings are **valid**. Raise your voice!

PRACTICE MAKES PROGRESS!

To express yourself, you can say:

"I need help with something."

"I've been feeling sad lately."

"I don't want to do that."

"I don't think that's fair."

GLOSSARY

bully: To bother or harm someone on purpose.

confidence: Believing in oneself.

consent: Permission or approval.

express: To make thoughts or feelings known by saying or writing.

eye contact: The act of two people looking at each other's eyes.

protect: To keep safe.

therapist: Someone who treats people with problems of the mind.

valid: Based on truth.

FOR MORE INFORMATION

BOOKS

Borgert-Spaniol, Megan. *Friends Support Each Other.* North Mankato, MN: Pebble Books, 2022.

McAneney, Caitie. *I Talk to Cope*. Buffalo, NY: PowerKids Press, 2023.

WEBSITES

Feelings Games

pbskids.org/games/feelings

Learn more about naming your feelings with these fun games.

Going to a Therapist

kidshealth.org/en/kids/going-to-therapist.html

Therapists can help you put your feelings into words. Read more about what therapy is like.

Publisher's note to educators and parents: Our editors have carefully reviewed these websites to ensure that they are suitable for students. Many websites change frequently, however, and we cannot guarantee that a site's future contents will continue to meet our high standards of quality and educational value. Be advised that students should be closely supervised whenever they access the internet.

INDEX